SPIRITUAL WHISPERS

SPIRITUAL WHISPERS

First Edition

BESTSELLING AUTHOR

DR. JAYÉ WOOD

SPIRITUAL WHISPERS

Published by Publish Your Gift®
An imprint of Purposely Created Publishing Group, LLC

Printed in the United States of America

ISBN: 978-1-64484-605-6 (print)
ISBN: 978-1-64484-606-3 (eBook)

ALSO BY DR. JAYÉ WOOD

Poetry

Platinum Love

Strength of a Woman

He is My High

Fiction

Cement Rainbow

DEDICATION

In Memory—

of my brothers: Douglas and Joseph; sister: Rosemarie; and niece: Patrice
May the present entire Wood and Lee family hear the Spiritual Whispers
of your life's learned lessons. Indeed, if one dares to not only hear but listen
and be guided accordingly by these **private angels!**

In Tribute—

of Madeline Albright: the first female secretary of state in American
history. Her legacy in the twentieth and twenty-first centuries is that of a
great champion of freedom for all people! A model for women now and
generations to come. Thus, inspiring, motivating, and making it clear that
women must not just have a seat at the table, but be an equal part of the
decision-making process as well. What an **EXTRAORDINARY** human
being who always exemplified leadership with **grace** and **dignity**.

Much Congratulations—

to Ketanji Brown Jackson: the first black woman to serve on the US
Supreme Court! Yes, after 232 years. But, unlike the lottery, luck had
nothing to do with it. Instead, it was deemed and so written by God that
this glass ceiling at this time, space, and place be shattered by this **amazing**
woman within the spirit of His holy whispers heard not only in America,
but around the world! Thus, we shall not only continue to stand upon the
"shoulders of slaves" but embrace diversities, equality, and unity for all
people consequently. **Rise, rise . . . rise!**

And to—

all of you: Be it aloud or within the spirituality of a whisper—regardless of your differences, country, nationality, faith, gender, LGBTQ2+, status, etc.,—I wish you His mighty guidance and blessings, and pray that you shall know and always hear

Him Saying—

Be kind (English); **être gentil** (French); **элдэг бай** (Mongolian); **Berbaik** (Indonesian); **Sei Freundlich** (German); **Vriendelik** (Afrikaans); **будь добрым** (Russian); **Bí cineálta** (Irish); **Amiable** (Spanish); **善待** (Chinese); **Legyen kedves** (Hungarian); **친절하게 대해** (Korean); **Sea gentil** (Portuguese); **Být milý** (Czech); **Sii gentile** (Italian); **να είσαι ευγενικός** (Greek); **Vær snill** (Norwegian); **親切にする** (Japanese); **Budite ljubazni** (Croatian); **бути добрим** (Ukrainian); **tử tế** (Vietnamese); **Dwe kalite** (Haitian), **Dayaalu hon** (Hindi), **Jẹ́ onínúure** (Yoruba); مہربانی (Urdu), and you . . . **etc., etc., etc.** Oh,

The Beauty—

of kindness—even when you do not know . . . another!

TABLE OF CONTENTS

PART TWO: ONLY YOU

ART THREE: HEART MELODIES

FOREWORD

. Jayé Wood's book *Spiritual Whispers* is **AWESOME!** I am eighty-two
ars old and the immediate spiritual connection that I felt with the poet as
e read the poems was like nothing I had ever experienced. Absolutely **IN-
REDIBLE!** Her **EXCEPTIONAL poetic voice** that is infused throughout
r poetry is a **gift** from God as she preaches and **masterfully** teaches about
ity, equality, kindness, and respect for all people . . . with a message for
genres, races, religions, sexes, etc., that flows through the **POWERFUL,
ROLIFIC, PROFOUNDNESS** of her **STRONG** yet **eloquent** poetic voice.

The words in this book are spiritual and deeply **intellectual** as Dr. Jayé
eaks to today's democracy and it's more than often hypocrisies. Likewise,
e addresses hatred, jealousy, naysayers, and the like . . . **encouraging** us all
rise above and become who God uniquely created each one of us to be.
us, accepting self with grace and integrity! How deep and thought-pro-
king is this message, particularly during these very chaotic and devastat-
times, not only in America but all over the world!

Dr. Jayé is also a **leader**! Yep, in my many years in the political arena
d leadership, her **unique** lyrical voice echoes a need and call for honest,
cent, fearless, and compassionate leaders with a charismatic spirit of do-
what is right for all humanity! Overall, throughout Dr. Jayé's poetry, she
courages us all to "let God in" and embrace His spiritual whispers to guide
and, thus, the ultimate wealth . . . shall be Him. Dr. Jayé is not only a **po-
c genus**, she is a **great woman of God** that unselfishly shares her **MAG-
IFICENT** gift of poetry and invites us all to make His holy journey with
ve and compassion for each other!

Yes, God is as is reflected in Dr. Jayé throughout her book *Spiritual Whi* *pers*! The author's very **influential** and **inspirational** poetry undeniably pr vides a path of **hopefulness** even in darkness. What a timely **blessing**. Wh a living **legacy** for us all—present and future generations—to behold an likewise, make a collective, universal, **positive difference** for all of Go creatures!

Doris J. Cammack-Spencer,
Recently Retired President and CEO, Southern Maryland Minority Cham ber of Commerce; Honorary Lifetime Appointment as Chairwoman Eme itus, Southern Maryland Minority Chamber of Commerce; Co-founder c Concerned Black Women of Calvert County Maryland; Honorary Docto ate Received at Sojourner-Douglass College, Baltimore, Maryland

PART ONE

BUTTERFLY TIME

INSUPPRESSIBLE

Visions

of a sunset

encircled . . . my

heart and through its

Eye

a striking . . . revelation

I saw my soul, felt . . . God's

spirit—and it was then, I

knew

without a

doubt—simply

insuppressible, that the

Continuance

of my life

must—and

will—include Him . . .

SIGNATURE

It

could have been, but

it never—materialized

Might

have happened . . . nonetheless

it never did should—have

Come

oh, well did—not and then

there's always . . . tomorrow

Places

times, things—indeed

the years we take for

Granted

quickly pass us by teaching—life's

lessons along the way of which we . . . seldom

Grasp

in their moments, one day you sign—on

yep, you got mail: God's . . . signature season to

You

suddenly, you know you—must change your priorities

fulfill empty dreams or reach for new—ones without

Hesitation

you, likewise, know you . . . must—live, enjoy and

appreciate His—graciousness and claim your life . . . now!

BUTTERFLY TIME

My

heart

bleeds—tears

My

soul

cries—pain

My

spirit whispers—peace

Today

I see . . . clearly

Tomorrow

I not only hear, but listen

Yesterday

indeed, butterfly time . . . and so

Now

I not only appreciate but, treasure—His

remarkability of each . . . moment and its seconds within that

I

still—fly lifted within the comfort of His . . . always unchanging love and

uidance . . . consequently, with each breath I—take: I shall forever be giving

Praise

to—Thee that I . . . continue in this time, space, and place

acefully echoing: Amen . . . Hallelujah and—surely, to God be the . . . Glory!

DIVINE WILL

This

place will not

steal—my soul, the

Reeking

of its . . . horrors

masked—beyond

Frightening

this place—is a murderer of

soul's . . . hopelessness, blindness, and

Ignorance

this place is ugly—a mastery

of . . . contempt, corruption, and

Evil

this . . . place for the sake

of God's . . . divine will—I

Survive

my blood . . . flows like

a river—accepting its

Warmth

my mind, body, spirit, and soul are now one—united

in harmony—with every awakening day and . . . I am

Grateful

rejoicing in His—name, outside this . . . place

each morning covered in His—grace: Yes, and I be . . . blessed!

SOMETIMES

Some

people can fake

a good life while never

relating to or telling . . . their

Truth

sometimes one may

suppress a memory, but

the stain—they cannot

Erase

sometimes they,

likewise, falsely believe

that they can even—bury a

Secret

oh, indeed their pain is seldom

hidden from . . . everyone and, thus, one must

eventually make a choice, to confront self and all it's

Hypocrisy

subsequently, understanding sometimes will never

be always, it is only . . . God that holds this—permanence

so, why not seek His love, peace, guidance—and grow beyond . . .

JOY

Joy of

life—speak to me

tell of love, if I will

Joy of

sadness . . . speak to me, tell

of how long—this I need

Joy of

pain . . . speak to me—tell

of hurt that I—bare

Joy of

fear . . . speak to me, tell

of tears—that I may clear

Joy of

despair . . . speak to me, tell of

faith and hope, that I may believe

Joy of

God . . . speak to me, tell of when,

of where, of now, of why, of truth

of—all

and—that

I—must . . .

RIGHT

Justice

hope, possibilities, and prosperity

will—prevail when people do the

Right

thing . . . so, remember you have

the—power to chart the course in a

Good

way for the next . . . generation by doing

right, knowing what is right and being—right to

Self

and others as reflected in God's—mightiness

so, let's come together . . . in unity my brothers, sisters, and

All

people as we move forward . . . putting Him

first with a pledge of allegiance to Thee our . . . Holy

Father

to restore . . . hope, nicety, and strive for

accepting, appreciating diversity, preservation, and

Inclusion

emember, time sometimes appears to—happen when you want it . . . oh

ıt, be not fooled and miss the present . . . opportunity to make a difference

Today

yes, hope starts with you . . . and is contagious when one puts

humanity first: What a blessed spread that needs no—vaccination!

PRIVATE ANGEL

(Dedicated to the Goods family and . . . you)

When

love has to leave

the here and . . . now

It

can be hard to

let go and move—on

Sometimes

it may even

be difficult—to

Understand

that when you

decide to let—go and

Move

on you take their love

with—you wherever you go

Permanently

residing in your . . . soul and spirit

as your very special private—**angel**

How

sweet indeed, when this blessing of . . . God's forever love is not only

realized, but embraced with a materialization of—eternity saying . . . I am her●

SNOWFLAKE

To

watch a snowflake . . . fall from

the heavens—feel its grace, light and

Weary

no particular destination—earth

bound it seems, not in a hurry

Riding

on the wind, all its shapes

so—distinct the instance it

Hits

the ground—living life as it

happens, undefined are her tears—yet

Defined

its fantasies—unrealized

much more than one could know—as

She

seems to say

it's—okay . . .

UNCAPTURED

Don't

I know you

florescent one—shiny

and bright—radiant in light

I

suspect you

possess unspoken powers

illuminating in—force

Intimacy

of cultivation

mingling of all dimensions

endless with countless—foe's

No

doubt you shall continue to

befuddle the minds of mere mortals who

continue to try and seize your—uncaptured

Being

oh, but the purity of

your . . . soul scares many who dare

to whisper even your name—in vain . . .

DEAR GOD

Upside

down what's it all mean—violence

within every corner in my . . . house

Surrounded

spears and fears

protection, myself—my child

Nothing

fits, a he or she

to give or take—to be or not

Changes

Dear God: Is this real

or has it always been—in

Eyes

that—now

see—through

Maturity . . .

GHETTO BIRD

I

look out at the ghetto—trash see his

leaves, feel its wind and smell her perfume

Hey

there girl, boy . . . walking that ghetto—road

here's a pole, fence upon which a ghetto—cat strolls

Alone

ghetto—dog barks

so loud—but walks real

Slow

up high ghetto—smoke, gray

skies and soon ghetto—rain will surely

Fall

in hope the ghetto . . . bird flies

low that he or she may claim all that

Remains

yet, as fate would have it

the ghetto—bum gets the

Crumbs

trees of barren color, nesting birds flock

together, because tomorrow another . . . shall

Fly

But

lower . . .

LOOKING GOOD

(Dedicated to Nick Cannon)

Just

maybe kindness, caring, hope, love,

and laughter are indeed . . . the keys to a healthy

longevity—consequently, causing one to always be looking

Good

regardless of their stage of . . . development, status, class, gender,

nationality, what they are wearing, their hairstyle, what they are driving, or

their difference of opinion . . . etc.

You

see, it's something about

the geniality of a smile that

exudes warmth, friendliness, and a

Safe

place for another to—breathe in spite of their

mood, present or past trials—tribulations, even if only for a

moment irrespective of their . . . attitude and when this happens

Awe

to witness the beauty of another's glow . . . because you

shared a genuine smile whether knowing or—unaware of their

circumstances or challenges . . . now that feels and looks—good on

Everyone

while it may only be for a minute or so: What dearness

to give. . . another so, always give praise not only each

day, but second, hour, and all in-between to . . . God when

You

have been given

the skill of evolution—within

causing an inner . . . elegance of light to

Shine

outward . . . thus, inspiring others to do the same, it's no—game

f one loves self, lives their most authentic . . . life not only doing the best

ey can but, going above and beyond to lift another: He—will gift . . . thee with

Multiplicity

yes—and

it shall . . . be

with a—smile!

ECHOES

My thoughts

ideas all so clear

I can, I will, and I shall

To be

to become . . . to continue

I must, I will, and I shall

To grasp

my dreams, to really

believe, to hold my hopes

I shall

I must, and I will . . . to give it time

to wait it out and to let . . . it flow

Have I

the time . . . to

say I must, but do that I don't

Why is

it that I—wait and when

I do, will it be . . . too late?

TRASH

Sometimes

trash may be tolerated

oh, but when it begins to smell

Bad

due to heightened

ongoing . . . negativity within—one's

Circle

be it family, friends, work, church, etc.,

do not fall prey to their draining . . . deranged

Jealousy

yes, this garbage has no defined pick-up date . . . thus, if you have

als you desire and are working to attain . . . you must—understand and be

Aware

of the possible damage of backstabbers and . . .wishy

washers that breed within the rubble . . . believing they are

Unseen

oh, but when you see the light, be like the . . . sheep when

they want to birth . . . they seek a quiet—place above the

Toxicity

so, step up . . . away from the—smelliness of

hatred, breathe a freshness and birth . . . your—dreams!

JUDGEMENTALITY

When

one is always—judgmental

of others . . . one day this judgementality

will be directed in great . . . force toward

Themselves

you see when a person's

dominant personality . . . is to

belittle, disgrace, judge, slander, and

Smear

the character of

others—undoubtedly, without

question, they will . . . eventually

Destroy

self, because

they forget, do

not know . . . or

Refuse

to . . . believe

that the—ultimate

judge—is God!

TOMORROW

Live

for the moment let . . . not

tomorrow come before its time

Reach

not back for

that which has

Gone

sounds like a . . . song that one could

enjoy for the moment maybe—unlike

Life

which hasn't just a . . . moment

nor the—luxury of wasted

Time

which we think we—control taking for

granted there will be . . . tomorrow, thus, choose to

Explore

only the moment, indeed need there . . . be

tomorrow for—some maybe not, for me

My

today's—hopes, aspirations, and dreams are

tomorrow and my yesterday's all—moments . . .

TIME

Sometimes

in life everyone will need at some point

to stop . . . think, breathe, exhale, and inhale even—when

there appears to be no—light and no way . . . out with much

Reservation

which often must take place not only on the outside but, within

as well, consequently equipping one with the strength to fully . . . shine lik

a—star while, maybe unbeknownst to them they already are . . . they just need t

Rise

up . . . in spite of any hesitation, you see when one refuses to move

on he or she also . . . stops the growth of self to fully—be all they can

so, just remember there are no perfect . . . people not even in the Bible: Sa

What

yes, some were liars, drunks, overweight, too tall, too

short suicidal, too old, day dreamers, broke, prostitutes,

murders, denied Christ, hypocrites and on and on . . . and yet,

within His light . . . they rose above so, next time you're soaking in

Excuses

hink of difficulties as realities . . . sometimes presenting problems that may

seem never ending, yet the ultimate realism of something that is...forever

is God's gifts of love . . . so, treasure this, take care of you and let not your

time to pause, be an excuse not to get—back in the game

Instead

keep the faith, show

up, embrace and praise—Thee

for your time . . . it's got your name on—it!

THE STORM

Hear

my—plea this

boat rocks to and fro

Now

I know my thirteen-

year-old may go astray

Her

heart fills with fire

and brings much desire

I

say without shame maybe

I am to—blame show me

How

a distance grows of . . . hate

and anger nourishes the flame

Trust

and respect loses tone while

rules are torn to—shreds the

Storm

will come and go but, this boat

I know shall—rock some more

Guide

Me

Lord . . .

SAY WHAT

I

am so—confused

about you . . . me, my child

How

can it be . . . this is

so much to conceptualize—I

Wish

in this time

and space . . . just

Maybe

I could start—it

all over again . . . then

Again

I would still be—bewildered

oh, if only I had the perseverance and

Persistence

of a butterfly, gracefully—I would fly

say what—Lord . . . "Spread your wings

And

you can" . . . and so, I did and now today, many years

later forever grateful to Thee . . . am I and—I continue to

Soar

with wings of—praise

gratitude, faith, and an always . . . Amen!

CIRCUIT BREAKER

It

is the eleventh hour and the—hour

glass is long past half full, instead it is near

Empty

and so, it's time to do something

different way—beyond any toxic

Leadership

instead, the onus is on those

who are enabling, fence riding, and

Sliding

naively thinking that by falsely . . . holding up and fronting

the poisonous one in charge will benefit—them, in spite of the

Rhetoric

disgrace, lack of ethics, no principles, back

stabbing, lying, and cheating . . . just—unconscionable

Damaging

so many, already hurting, afraid, praying, hoping for a miracle

and the like . . . maybe—you will get the position, house, car, etc.

Gifts

as desired for your selfish performance—unlike the circuit breaker who

ps up without any personal interest: Knows she or he does not stand alone

What

a badge of—honor

what a legacy, what a Holy—Spirit when and if: To . . . behold!

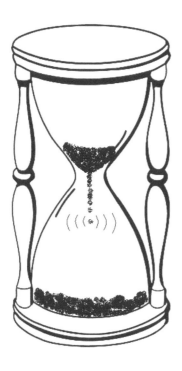

(((☺)))

DIVINES

Have

you ever thought

or . . . wished

If

today could be—tomorrow and

just maybe for a moment . . . stand

Still

well, as I reflect on my life—there have

certainly, been times when I have . . . hypothesized

What

if today . . . might have been yesterday—and then

through maturation . . . I now realize if all this were

Possible

how would I know or even begin—to

appreciate—today's joys, life's challenges, and the

Eloquence

of—His spiritual entwinement . . . with

my mind and body, spirit and soul . . . oh, indeed—I

Pray

that I may always . . . know God's—love

at each arising . . . and wish not it be frozen, but instead

Treasure

the beauty of Thy—divines

in its—moments every . . . today!

DEHYDRATED

Some

are asking why people

seem so angry during these times which

are complicated even more with an—ongoing

Pandemic

societal divide with disrespect for

differences of voices, complexions, class, status, and the

like resulting in brutality, protest, lootings, shootings, killings

Hurting

everyone, particularly the innocent who are now

dying twice as much, suffering economically—unable

to feed themselves, their families, or maintain businesses

Thirsty

are the people, filled

with despair—worrying simply

desperate and nearing . . . dehydration

Change

in the midst of this . . . storm is not only

needed in leadership and law enforcement

but, within—ourselves as well, thus, we must

Encourage

local people and others to get involved . . . feel the

anxiety of people—everywhere who do not know when

or if the end will come: Enough, let's do it now . . . with

God's

grace and mercy,

subsequently, a

rising of—hopefulness!

SAVING GRACE

When

your well . . . runs dry

who will quench—your

Thirst

warm your—winter, cool your summer

sun, and clear your leaves in order to

Welcome

your spring, indeed, when one believes—need not ask these

questions: No mystery, the answer is clear . . . it shall be the one and only

God

Thy mightiness . . . always just in time Savior

yes, your saving grace is He bearing fruit as only... He

Can

be it winter, fall, spring, or summer

like the beauty and wisdom of a butterfly . . . a

Smile

where there was worry, pain, wavering hope, or feeling alone

suddenly there is optimism, joy, peace, and a reassurance of His

Love

thus, praising and thanking: Him whether aloud or amidst a whisper is

all one's spirit needs do: Oh, the sweet sound of—Amen, Amen . . . Amen!

PLAY ON

Life's

like—a

card game

Sometimes

low and other times high

you win, you—lose and you

Play

on, if not today

then tomorrow and each

Day

thereafter, and

when—the

Hand

grows weary—you could give in

but—then there's always the

Game

yes, eventually you must . . . play the hand

so, choose wisely this play is—yours . . .

PART TWO

ONLY YOU

PRAISE

Monday

I thought, today I begin—then

Tuesday

I knew with hope I could, but now it's

Wednesday

I will think—some more and

Thursday

the road I—travel starts at the end

Friday's

like an eagle flying strong with

Purpose

and yet, I must learn and know the

Wisdom

of the owl and the resilience of the butterfly

Hustle

bustle . . . too tired—for Saturday's ball, then praise: Thee Sunday and

Tomorrow

as is His will—I begin again . . . understanding not to take for

Granted

a job is just a . . . job: Instead, a pearl of hope when there is—faith!

LIFE

Life

is who you . . . are

Life

is who you . . . love

Life

is how you . . . give

Life

is your . . . compassion

Life

is your . . . kindness

Life

is your . . . family

Life

is your . . . friendships and fellowships

Life

is your . . . humbleness

Life

is your . . . courage

Life

is your . . . persistence to speak and stand for—rightness

Life

is your ability to . . . empower for—good

Life

is embracing yourself in—totality to include one's . . . truths

Life

is believing in something greater . . . than your opportunities

Life

is your . . . experiences to include the complexities of the journey

Life

is respecting . . . differences

Life

is appreciating . . . both nature and humanity

Life

is a holy . . . celebration regardless of its—challenges

Life

is the eloquence of God's . . . love shining within—without

Life

is the essence of one's heart, soul and spirit in

Harmony

with—His heavenly will!

ONE

Of

courage, confidence

fairness, peace, love . . . and

Compassion

we are all—one with a . . . predetermined

holy mission of hoping, sharing, caring, and having

Faith

giving thanks . . . be the

gifts large or—small

Believing

in prayer—when sincere

thus, remember to speak

Acknowledge

either winning or

conceding—do it with

Grace

recognizing you, me, him, her . . . need no—DNA test, regardless

of our differences, diversities, imperfections, or perfections

Yes,

ollectively we are all . . . God's creatures connected universally and spiritually

ecause of that first divine . . . breath we all received from our Holy—Father

Related

ndeed, via His . . . seeds from Heaven and so, be—kind to each other and

emember: just as thy supremacy giveth thee its first breath . . . so too, will

He

determine if . . . how, when,

and even where—we shall go . . .

SHADOWBOXING

Some

people spend their entire life

shadow . . . boxing in a ring all by

themselves, delivering perishing, piercing

Punches

to the right, left, and all in-between while

the hits appear to bounce—back they feel

nor see no visible signs that they have been

Struck

falsely convincing . . . themselves that they can and will—destroy anyone who

dares to step to their wrongness, unbeatable they—brag believing no

one can catch them, much like a game the little child plays when first

Discovering

their shadow: Laughing, jumping up and down, trying to

hit it or step on this thing, then running, thinking it is chasing

them, likewise, believing they are faster, smarter, thus, will . . . not be

Caught

oh, how sweet this childish game, which for most

at least we hope—fades with maturity, reminding

us that our shadows are reflections of self, a mirror of

Truth

should we dare look—beyond its exterior . . . nowhere to run or hide, we

cannot escape instead, only with courage, decide to recognize, accept, repent, and

accountable with a commitment to grow in God's—light even when we do not

Always

see the—shining of His forever . . . brilliance believers know

He—is at all times present and will never forsake thee . . . anybody

home: If so, can you hear me exalting God's name over all evil with

Mercy

praise—be Thy name, hallelujah be Thy Holy Spirit and: Glory

be to Thee for endlessly being just a whisper—above with no numbers

remember, no cell phones, computers, or other technology needed, just a

Permanent

connection without any shadows

no holding, waiting time, or voicemail

requesting leave a message, oh well . . . to merely talk about how

Good

this be . . . is not enough, instead understanding, embracing

and respecting how: Great this godly—heavenly majesty of

His—love truly be for us all consequently, causing one of faith and

Trust

to . . . sincerely

shout in the—dearest

of appreciation: Amen and . . . Thank you!

ONLY YOU

The

way your life is and has been

for so long has now become normal

for everyone else as well the—drama

Sensationalism

that surrounds your world . . . is—Oscar material

but there is no applause, no standing ovations or big

deals at least, not for you—instead it's like you are

Sliding

down a mountain, speeding, hurtling, plunging out

of control, yep—you need help, but you won't ask, can't ask

you need to yell or beg for support or forgiveness, but you

Don't

and as always someone might catch you, break your

fall, and sit you up straight again, only this time I am

hoping not, even though it hurts to watch, I—pray you hit rock

Bottom

hard as hell, face to face . . . with your

demons of whom you have given your soul

yes, no one, nothing, only—you can decide your

Fate

hopefully, you will free your . . . crying

spirit who sometimes—dares to even hint,

dream, or breathe the thought of a new—day . . .

TAILORED

Actions

have consequences . . . thus, as one grows

we must think independently of leads we

Acquiesced

when we were children, teenagers, or young adults

and for some . . . far beyond if—ever you see the true

Essence

of maturity . . . is becoming our own beings regardless of differences to

include not being liked by others when we refuse to compromise self:

Fit

in just to get

along, yet faking a

Good

Look of a smile some may sadly join the group: Well, God designed a

specific style . . . just for you: Thus, it is merely a myth, sales—pitch at

Best

that one size

fits . . . all so, if you

Dare

to show up with individuality, uniquely—flaunting your tailor fitted

confidence, determination, or resilience the runway is and

Will

be—yours

with—endless

Opportunities

alk about dressed to the nines . . . try a ten and remember to—always give

od the praise and simply be you . . . I heard everyone else is already taken!

UNSTOPPABLE

Don't

wait for somebody

else to empower you, the

best is yet to come—so

Be

kind to yourself

do not listen to

haters instead, surround

Yourself

with positive people

and only share your

dreams—accordingly

Remember

hopefully, with maturity

comes strength, thus, desired

goals can be achieved—at any level

Should

you really—want and have an unstoppable . . . attitude

resilience, self-compassion, openness with vulnerability: Wow . . . look out

you will not only achieve your destiny and live your purpose,

but you will own it as well!

A THOUGHT

Sometimes

I just sit and stare

Sometimes

I just sit and travel

Sometimes

I just sit and listen

Sometimes

I just sit and whisper

Sometimes

I just sit and think—why am I

Sometimes

I just sit stuck in a . . . thought

Sometimes

I just sit, wonder, and—be . . .

ENDLESS ROAD

Well

my Lord the time

has come—again we must

Talk

this child forever grows worse

yes, a seed I gave birth—I no longer

Know

believe or trust—where do I go

from here, how do I start, oh indeed—I am so

Tired

my mind wearies the—tears of my heart

which fills its capacity and I have . . . not the

Strength

to travel what appears

an endless road—another mile

What's

that—you

say—Lord

Ok

thanks—for

being there, now I—can . . .

SHATTERED

When

dreams are torn

with shattered . . . wings, the

Sun

doesn't shine—and the wind

pushes . . . through, sometimes hard to

Find

a . . . breath

of—fresh

Air

and then

as I . . . begin to

Breathe

Awe . . . it is only

the softness—of His

Voice

that cools

my soul—and

Inspires

my spirit—to move on, stay

on, reach on, and . . . so, I—do!

NO MORE

(Dedicated to my younger self)

Many

years ago, when I called you . . . friend and—you

called me best, what a bond we developed, at least I thought

unlike any we had known and as we grew or was it as I—developed

Never

did you support—unless

of benefit to you, not ever did you

compliment—except . . . if an advantage to you, instead

loudly

applauding when I failed or slipped, all this—I

have known—and yet, I have played along I—suppose

I wanted or thought . . . I needed you as a friend, if only in

Name

yes, I have tried

by giving you your own medicine

instead, it made me sick . . . while

Even

in the presence of my dearest loved

ones—you have displayed the same toward

me always with a front of a smile, chuckle, or

Laugh

well, of this game I have grown tired, to end once

before I—tried, but now I not only must, but know

that I can, thus, no longer can I or will—I call you

Friend

and disregard your obvious

negativity, envy, jealousy, and the

like, whatever the need I—felt before

No

more . . . yes, it feels good to know, whatever

the magnetism that drew me to your obvious

charade of—friendship is no more, not only have I

Grown

but, oh my sweet Jesus—I thank you

for guiding me not to feel or wish bad

for the one, I once called friend . . . and so, today to them

I

merely say with

your . . . grace and mercy

without any . . . harshness: Good—bye!

FALSE FACE

So

where's your Bible

have you . . . prayed

where's

the church—have you attended

where's the love, have you really

Cared

how dare you stare with your false

face and judge another, if you—do your

Reflection

will surely glare for all

to know and point in—blissful

Shame

of how you have—falsely risen

attempting to—sour that of pure love and faith

Behind

a mask—of

hate and pain . . .

AFRAID

When

one is afraid of something

within—they tend to blame others

by making them the target of their own

imperfections, shame, disgust, and insecurities

They

falsely convince

themselves that they are

the brightest, a shining star

even in the darkest of rooms

Afraid

they become driven, obsessed, filled

with dangerous and destructive jealousy

toward anyone who dares to achieve their dreams

and be recognized with praise, joy, and congratulations

How

sad and lonely it must truly be

to live one's life under a constant

mask of self-hatred . . . how much easier

it would be just to . . . be God's gift—you!

FLIP

Sometimes

in life one . . . must flip the

script—yes, time to move on leaving

Behind

the ratchet . . . naysayers and their cowardly,

gutless, spineless, un-spiritual . . . behaviors toward

You

for being who you are

who God . . . created you to

Be

shining far above their self-loathing and unfortunate self

inflicted—unhappiness . . . which they try to project upon you, and so

Introspection

as you change the script with—kindness is a must and

yes, this will surely leave them wondering—how in the . . . hell

Your

light not only continues to—shine but, gets even . . . brighter

with each day and sometimes mere seconds, minutes are the

Flashes

oh, if only they knew . . . when one sincerely believes and gives

Him all the praise . . . they too, can not only grow—beyond their evils, but

Enjoy

he goodness—His almighty has waiting just for thee so, if indeed you need to

p the script why not do it now: Go ahead, I—dare you to grow above and . . . beyond!

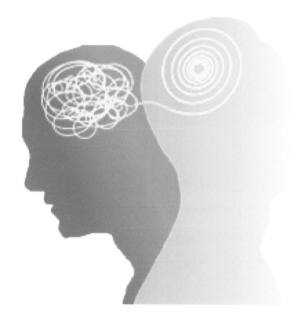

SPEAK VICTORY

Whatever

you constantly

say . . . it

will become your

Reality

nobody likes me . . . well, I am not this, not that,

can't do that . . . this—too short, too tall, too fat, too

small, my hair, skin, face, race, gender, etc., etc., etc.

Complaints

far too many people . . . spend their entire

lives comparing themselves to others and what they

do not have, believing—they will never have and can't have

Developing

a life of hopelessness, faithlessness

unless they can begin to . . . speak victory to

self and acquire a true belief in—God coupled with a

Transformation

of attitude . . . with not only a willingness

to be all that they can, but a commitment

to . . . self to do the work, embrace the challenges and

Personify

a new . . . self and

talk that—echoes

I can, I am . . . I will!

ATONEMENT

Far

too often people exhibit acts of

bad behavior . . . be they physical or

verbal toward others, because of their

Differences

in complexion, gender, language, sexual orientation, etc.

and with an audacity, some justify these behaviors

by saying he or she was just being flippant . . . just a

Joke

oh, and yeah . . . when they strike or

attack others who appear so unlike them . . . they

may say . . . well they deserved it shucks, they don't

Belong

in . . . here

walking—around

like—they own something and bedsides when they are

Speaking

they could be cussing me out heck: I don't—know what they are

saying . . . talking like that, looking—like that wonder where they

are from, how did they get in here anyway, while . . . simultaneously

Cowardly

soliciting chuckles and laughs

toward those labeled . . . odd, often with

unambiguous, derogatory, and demeaning . . . behaviors

Well

I could go on and on . . . instead, to you who are

listening and want to do better . . . be better, help another do

the same—remember we are all human beings . . . which includes

Diversity

thus, what you do not understand . . . ask

instead of throwing feces upon another—which

may backfire . . . yep, causing one to step in their own

Foulness

you see, God's . . . atonement is a guaranteed

consequence of hatred and violence toward

His—children . . . and overall universe, so make sure your

Life

that you live

are—mirrors and

not just—windows . . .

BEHOLD

As

the old saying goes

the apple does not fall far from

the . . . tree whether good or—bad

Wonder

if this is still a

belief today and

does it always hold

True

you see, in my life

I have witnessed a bad—tree with

abused, affected, and just rotten generational apples

And

then low and behold—though

perchance just a few, some—do indeed fall

far from the tree, ultimately deciding to travel a

Different

journey, while bruised as well as maybe

feeling afraid, alone, frightened, pain . . . and even

patronized for having the nerve to stray—away from the

Tree

and yet, it is this courage that

empowers one with determination not to be

a fallen apple—tied to a sick tree, and when they

Prevail

taller and stronger than the

tree itself . . . you may often hear from

family and others: Oh well, they were

Unlike

us—they, may not really be related, shucks

they looked and acted different, they had that, they

think—they are better or maybe . . . they were just

lucky

when in reality, not only did this apple come from . . . the same

tree, but refused to merely—accept the adage of fallen apples

consequently, decided to shine their own brightness and, thus, allowed

God

to gleam through their soul and spirit

subsequently, guiding and shining His light for them to be

and behold their true—purpose with love, faith, and kindness . . .

GESTALT

Even

without talking

negatively to another

person . . . negative thoughts

Damage

oneself—thus, when one

can and does blind themselves

to verbal . . . or silent ranting and

Raving

about someone—else just

maybe they make possible a clear

space to truly see . . . self and embrace its

Revelation

toward a positive transformation

yes, a gestalt of feelings . . . of love, kindness, and goodness

with a—hopefulness exposing confidence . . . thus, allowing the

Wholeness

of self to be far

more powerful and open to

God's awaiting—greatness just for . . . You!

FRESH AIR

Every

now and then, one must get out of their own

way as well as—that of others in order for

Progress

to happen—you see, true

leaders know when to allow

Fresh

air to enter—consequently embracing different, clear,

and realistic thought processes with . . . sound—possible

Alternatives

yet, when the pompous one flaunts the title leader and

fails to do this they—endanger the lives of others and

Society

yes, today more than ever, we need—leaders

who are caring with servility, compassion, and

Humanity

thus, in order for a new—day to not only

happen, but flourish we must—not fall for the

Okie–Doke

instead, we must vote for and demand—authenticity of

leadership, that not only talks the talk, but also walks—the talk!

TRANSFORMATION

Good

can push . . . forward

kindness, compassion, and

even an embrace of . . . differences

You

see . . . mindfulness starts

with—self, consequently

in order to bring . . . about

Change

in others one must . . . first

evaluate—self even if perceived

as successful there may still . . . be a

Void

of emptiness, self—centeredness

loneliness, pretense, and overall

unhappiness, so remember one of the

Greatest

relationships are those that have a spiritual . . . connection as its

foundation . . . subsequently, when this happens, we become not only

ronger, but fearlessly shielded by God's—faith and will indeed . . . make a

Positive

difference illuminating . . . kindness,

heartiness, gentleness, acceptance, and love

for all His florae regardless of their roots, statures,

Colors

zip codes, status, strengths, weaknesses . . . etc. Thus, together

with respect, appreciation, genuine care, embracement, protection,

and nourishment for each other we will all—grow and behold a . . . self

Transformation

while unbeknownst to some, that we already hold the key: Go ahead,

)en the door . . . Wow! What a display of blooms and all we need do now:

continue to flower ahead and enjoy the beauty of His—flowers everywhere!

POET MAN

Voice

of song—raving

of charm, harmony, and

Peace

still flows when

you speak—untarnished

Unblurred

take my hand, let me

lead, this you—said long ago

Poet

man, without a castle, tree without

bark, river without water, child—without

Love

share with me

this wealth—of

Power

show . . . beyond its

looking glass—that I may

Engulf

upon—its

mountains—and valleys . . .

KNOWLEDGE

In

all that I

know . . . of all

I shall—know

I

know . . . not

where—forth I

grow . . . tomorrow's

Dreams

which are of the past

indeed, yesterday's hopes

and . . . today's—presence

Undefined

and so, I continue to

search, wonder, and even ponder

for the ultimate . . . knowledge

Yes

a—particular

phenomena—called

absolute—wisdom!

EXHILARATION

When

you love—you somebody will too, like floating on

ice, cool, easy, real nice . . . a winner at life your—paradise

You

cannot lose snow, blizzards,

rainstorms, hurricanes, avalanches—pure

Sunshine

every day's a

treasure—all steps a

Climb

and each

dream you . . . touch

Singing

dancing, flaunting, and strutting

an untainted—exhilaration . . . of

Love

for self, thy—holiness

and divines of . . . Him!

PINCH ME

Just

being alive, knowing there is hope

and sharing this with—others during

Today's

sometimes doom and

gloom is—indeed a

Blessing

you see, even in the darkness, I am

never alone or bored as long as I—have

God

with His constant love, guidance, and assurance

I can always find a smile, share some joy, and be

Optimistic

and so, if ever there is even a . . . hint

of evilness . . . attempting to invade my—space like a

Divine

intervention: Bam! A pinch me . . . moment

surfaces just in—time dominating my total

Being

lifting me higher, while simultaneously empowering my soul and spirit to

continue in His amazing—glory and so, with much praise and grace I . . . do

LETTING GO

Letting

go can be hard

oh, but when it causes you

Stress

it can bring you down, sling

you around and lay you flat—while

Hurting

your heart, stealing your

soul and damaging—your

Spirit

so, why not take back your control—yes, do

it now, no more headaches, sleepless nights, etc.

Make

the next Lyft driver you call be—God

no cash, credit, or debit cards needed . . . just

Belief

and as advertised: His rides are

safe with a guarantee . . . to deliver!

PART THREE

HEART MELODIES

THANK YOU

If

you—think about it

age is a matter of the

Mind

if you don't

mind . . . it doesn't

Matter

as . . . cliché as

it may be—the

Profoundness

is in the mind, so to

you, I simply say . . . be

Kind

always to yourself—and greet each day

with a smile, an open heart, amazement, and

Wonder

shouting: Thank you sweet Jesus, my God

and Lord—I Am . . . Hallelujah! Hallelujah! Hallelujah!

DADDY

(Honorably Awarded Five Battle Stars in World War Two)

Sweet

gentle, kind, and considerate, his strength

seldom seen and yet, I now know it was his strong

point that propelled him through his daily—trials and

Tribulations

indeed, some saw Daddy as

weak, clearly unaware or

uncaring of his—weaknesses, surely, they

lacked

the knowledge to understand his

circumstance, or maybe it was the old adage that

persists even today: He's the breadwinner, provider, the

Man

such a load did Daddy carry, to include the scars and pains of a war

he honorably fought for his country yet, never a word would he

mutter, not even once did he complain at least not to

His

children, such

a—man

and now the

Weight

has been lifted, his face cracks a smile as

peace surrounds the calmness of his body and soul

simultaneously our spirts connect and I hear his kind

Whispers

do not be sad my child I shall—always

be a part of you my love, my heart, for I

have only laid here to rest—as is God's will, I am

Complete

then quickly without hesitation, as if we both were in the

here and now, I respond: A part of you—Daddy, I too

shall endlessly be and my heart will not be sad instead, within my

Soul

and spirit the love

we shared shall never

die, for I will forever—be

Daddy's

girl, you see—I love you

yesterday, today, and tomorrow—with the eternality of

His—holy grace, mercy, and beauty: And so, I salute . . . you!

LIFELINE

Today

this family . . . pains

and tomorrow—unable to

stay afloat—a lifeline may die

We

must at this very . . . critical

time forget our whining—blood

runs deep and the sharks are plentiful

Together

our hands

are very strong

a history of—struggles

Survival

perseverance, resilience

so, hold on—you to

me, to him, to her, and

United

in love, faith, belief

with God's divine . . . guidance

we will—make the journey!

I BELIEVE

Who

is He, where

is He—why is

He

surely, I don't know

for—I've never seen or heard Him

But

I believe, even though

I cannot see, hear, or touch

Him

I know—He

hears—me

I

think of Him as no...... color, instead as

someone to worship as He truly is—because I

Believe

and, yet I now ask myself—why can't I see, hear, or

touch Him—maybe He's just not ready for me to see Him, but

Gee

when and if that day should ever come, I wonder

would I be considered special, you know like—God!

BLUE ROSES

Sometimes

I feel as though they never had a chance oh, I know . . . I am guilty

of saying we all had the—same and maybe you too . . . feel or have felt

this way, but I now—know it's not so much an even . . . start instead, the

Embodiment

of one's strength, will, desire, and commitment

to not only embrace the journey, but do the work in order

to rise above the status quo and yet, just maybe when they

Feel

no . . . one prepared them

for the rough spots, shattered dreams

broken glass and cold hearts, blame will be their

Comfortable

game well, I could say . . . I wish this or that but, wishes are

for people foolishly wishing on a

star, kissing a frog, having a rabbit's foot, tossing pennies in

a pond, or caressing what they

believe to be a lucky charm, waiting for the gold to

magically appear . . . consequently, the

Reality

the tragedy of blue roses everywhere not . . . motivated, not inspired, and

ot cared about, thus . . . how can they—pull themselves up on bootstraps that

ey do not have . . . will you share or give them—yours, if not, the petals of blue

Roses

may . . . never

fully blossom even

when seasons peak a bit of

Hope

they will remain unmoved, unenthusiastic, trapped

in their—own shadows living a drama, self-inflicted and

yet, their hidden voices I believe God . . . hears and when they are

Truly

ready, declaring their sincerity to be

elevated, outside their self-pity then so, too, will

He—guide, equip, protect, and ensure them a new . . . beginning!

HEART MELODIES

A

man, whose castle

and throne shattered

Hopes

and—dreams

diminished, faith and beliefs

Weakened

and treated accordingly by many was he

but, deep within while very young, I—knew my

Dad

was quite a—man as he often shared

his aspirations, dreams, thoughts, and ideas with

Me

not doing as he, but to rise above and go beyond

yes, even though sometimes unsober, he never stuttered

Soft

was his speech, silent were his tears, barely above his whispers . . . reflective

of his strength, power, intellect, wisdom, logic, rationality, calmness, and

Peace

thus, with much heightened maturity today

I say unequivocally—quite a man was my dad, a

Philosopher

was he—never stoop lower than you

aspire and others shall not view you as such

Give

not and you shall receive not, always remember who you are

even after you've achieved, because

True

success shall be in who you are, yes, my

dad was quite a—man and to him I now write

Dear

Dad, I love you so—undoubtedly, I've been

cruel, a victim of not sharing that which I

Felt

I have been selfish, for much of who you were—I am

hear my praises, they are my heart melodies of—joy

Love

pride, respect, and appreciation for doing the best

you could with where you were—and who you were . . . well

I

made—it

Thank—you!

FOOT SOLDIERS

Long

ago, nearly a decade or more it seems I heard

someone speak of—war and foot soldiers, and now as if

Time

has stood still or taken me back, the spirit of these

words revisit my mind . . . a call for foot soldiers, and so today I

Ask

where are the foot

soldiers—surely, we are in a

War

in which

there can be no

Victory

unless its warriors

are those of lesser

Ranks

then and only then—do

we stand a fighting

Chance

for the enemy is strong

and grows powerful with each

Awaiting

day, its only—source of

energy is the infiltration of the

Human

mind and body, and the—dependence

of you and me to multiply its increasing

Demand

for supply is reality, so you see

we must take . . . heed to the words of the

Wise

we need not—colonels or

generals to defeat this beast, but a

Unitedness

of foot—soldiers in faith, hope

and will . . . courageously taking—charge

Dignifying

their commitment, because—if we

continue to ignore, hide, rationalize, and

Jeopardize

we shall surely fall

with the blood of thy—children's

Souls

on our—hands tell yourself no lies today or

we—die or at least our spirits, without even a whisper . . .

YOUR GLORY

I

remember so clearly the days when

I felt, it would never be—my golden

Star

planets afar—then a couple of days ago, the

voice on the phone asked—still interested, if so, it's

Yours

while I tried to contain my exhilaration . . . I could

hear yells and screams from deep within the depths of my—spirit

Wow

I thought—today is

surely, tomorrow—I've

Dreamed

all my steps, suddenly jumps and yet my talents

are small, no match for Thee—God who I know has

Bestowed

this greatness upon my soul and because of

this—I shall always be dancing to Your glory

How

wonderful—indeed: Is the splendor of God's love with it's always just

in time blossoms . . . shining brightly with inspiration, energy, and a

Lifting

of one's spirit

and soul as

He

has so graciously given me in this moment

and so, it is to Thee that—I give all the . . . praise!

SPIRITUAL WHISPERS

Just

as sure as love, day, and night

within the depths of my—spiritual whispers

I

used to wonder—why does it come, when

does it happen, and—where will it occur

Like

a rift from a job, cold

that's the flu—war that was

Peace

will I be ready, will there be pain

funny, today—I need nor desire

Answers

have no . . . questions

only—on and

On

shall—I

go, and to

Thee

that—I go

Amen! Amen! Amen!

THE BEAUTY

Sometimes

relationships fail or never

even begin because of the absence

of sincere—openness, invitingness, and

Receptiveness

allowing one to be seen

for who they are while—simultaneously

welcoming their voice, not only—hearing, but

Listening

oh . . . the beauty: Yes, the sweet sound of, I

heard you—without . . . prejudice, no blame, no

games, and no shame—just an illumination of . . . unselfish

Love

and

I

am—here . . .

GOD'S LOVE

Without

you . . . to talk—to

laugh with and share

my—life seems . . . so

Empty

I need—you to say

don't worry . . . I need to see

the emotions in your—face, I

Need

to reach out . . . and

for you to respond oh . . . baby

my darling—my love . . . it will be

Okay

and then, like a melody straight from

Heaven so . . . powerful was Thy presence

connecting our beings . . . reiterating and confirming that when one's

Heart

cludes God's love it is . . . undying and so, the voice said: Need not worry

you can, you will, and I—shall always be right here . . . now sleep

ight my love and thank—Thee with a forever praise and so, I . . . did and

Today

I am beyond okay—I am grateful with an

verlasting—gratitude for these memories of a special love and the power

His—whispers that gifted me such a priceless: Eternal treasure . . . Amen!

WEARY

(Dedicated to Mom)

Today

I watched a tired

and weary—soul on

Her

face years suddenly

appeared—her

Talk

unsure—stuttering

questions—thoughts

Redundant

far between were

her present or past

Memories

side by side we stood,

walking, laughing, holding hands, and

Sharing

her favorite chocolate

shake—yet I felt her loneliness and

Aloneness

of failing health which also

exhibited itself in her inability—to keep

Stride

as we strolled along—while some others

seemed not to notice, care, or were in denial, my

Heart

and mind began to fill with quiet—love

and forgiveness, while I did . . . not say out loud

I

Love

You

My

spirit kissed her . . . soul—spontaneously

we—hugged and as if she had . . . heard my

Whispers

she—smiled at me

and said: I love you—too...!

THE SHOW

Today

as we gather in remembrance, silent

are the cries of some while, others mere

sniffles appearing to hold—back and . . . then the

Shocking

overwhelming, out of place

laughter of a few family members

as the pastor attempts to speak of

God's

will and love

shocking—indeed

and then there were those

Screaming

shouting, jumping up

down and literally . . . falling

passing out—thus, hard to tell . . . what is

Fake

or real, particularly when they did not

show up when—needed, when they could see, feel

and know their earthly presence . . . oh well, as I watched the

Show

continually increasing in . . . drama, my mind

reflected upon something someone once told me

or—maybe I read . . . the body dies, but one's soul

Lives

on and can possibly occupy—another

being, how spiritual, how powerful, is

God . . . I silently thought and with much

Reassurance

I stood, walked with His grace to not only speak in

celebration of this life, but upon conclusion . . . toward the shell of

the body I strolled, gently . . . kissing her and immediately, my soul was

Empowered

as my spirit . . . lifted me with a melody of praise to sweet—Jesus

hat I am and continue to have—faith in . . . Him, consequently, elevating

me above the shamelessness of the show: Glory . . . Glory . . . Hallelujah!

INHALE/EXHALE

When

people can

inhale/exhale

Together

allowing the whispers

or their—spirits to

Connect

awe . . . it can be the beginning

of healing—their broken

Hearts

while at the same time opening—space to

begin the process of discarding the layers . . . of

Pain

oh, surely the wounds—sometimes

have festered for a while . . . maybe even

Years

nevertheless, when one allows another

to breathe in unison the feelings of being . . . alone

lessen

and together with God's civility and love—should they not

only believe, but welcome the dawning of a new breath—it will be . . .

SWEET MUSIC

I

felt its presence, uninvited

unwelcomed—unknown in my space

Frightened

I screamed; my soul—disturbed then quickly

my spirit regathered itself, awe—slowly she

Breathes

as—I lay transformed to another state

of mind, surveying my surroundings—I

Compose

myself replaying as best I—can and

to the sound of sweet . . . music her holy—breath

Caresses

me and instead, of

fear, I now feel—peace . . .

LET HIM IN

Ever

tried to convince your—self

of a needing a love long . . . gone

Sour

well, once during my . . . developmental

years, I had such a conversation with—my

Heart

that went something like: I know the passing will

come long before this moment's—existence ceases to

Be

I know when I have stopped loving. . . you

I'll be loving you and yet, the windows of . . . my heart seem

Shattered

and the—chill is cold while I know . . . or

maybe just feel—life without you would be

Lonely

in spite of your sometimes—shrewd and very cruel ways . . . which

may never... change I know or maybe just think, want to believe, or fill a

Void

when I have stopped loving you: within

my heart, I'll still be loving you . . . oh—God I

Pray

please help me . . . and then suddenly—there was this gentle

breeze, sweeping the broken . . . glass from beneath my feet with such

Tenderness

subsequently, I could now—stand and

walk without any fear or pain . . . thus, on this

Day

not lacking any hesitation, regret, shame, or

blame I knew . . . I must go and it was because—of a

Whisper

from far above—that I not only

heard but listened to—oh, the beauty of

God's

spirituality . . . yes, this one thing today—I

know for sure when we let Him . . . in the

Authenticity

of His—love will not only show . . . up as a beacon of light

but, fluorescently guide thee through the—darkness with

Grace

strength—and love

indeed: Hallowed be Thy... name!

BECAUSE

At

night when I cannot sleep,

instead of counting sheep

I

count my—blessings and

they begin with—Your

Almightiness

You are absolutely, unequivocally

explicitly . . . wonderful and each day—my life

Enriches

because of—You, thus, to know

You is—love, joy, peace, trust, and that

I

am—loved and to You: Thy awesome God, I give

Praise! Praise! Praise!

MAYBE

Maybe

we should—have spent

more . . . time knowing each other

Accepting

compromising, sacrificing, and . . . believing

maybe . . . we should not have—tempted

Reality

turning our backs on its . . . consequences

and yet, just—maybe seems too big . . . of a

Word

oh well, maybe

tomorrow . . . we will know less

Pain

and then again . . . maybe shall be exactly what

it is: You see even a . . . maybe is on God's—time!

THE FOREST

Somedays

it's as . . . cool as

the forest breezes

soft pillows of leaves

Embraces

the . . . serenity of ease

a harvest rainbow . . . I hear the

desert grows near—as Ms. Bluebird

Gently

graces—my ear

but . . . today, the forest seems

tight, rumpled in the shadows . . . as rainbow

Tears

reflect upon the—sun, while the desert grows nearer and

so, too . . . unafraid I go within the rhythm of God's amazing,

unconditional grace—love and guidance . . . awe, what serenity: What

Brilliance

what magnificence, what majesty is the

splendor and glory of Thy—spirituality just above a

whisper saying: I am here to be—hold and so, I do!

BEYOND

How

sweet—God's love

intoxicated, am I

When

I think of His kindness

faithfulness and belief in—me, how

Flattering

this cup—flows and

though it may sometimes

Overflow

never do I waste or take

for—granted instead, my body

Shivers

while instantaneously causing

my soul and spirit to twine and I—become

Immersed

in profound . . . gratitude

yet, my gratefulness is—beyond

Recognition

sometimes my spirit may whisper . . . indebtedness to Him and

other times shouts hallelujah, with an always: Praise of thankfulness!

HALLELUJAH

Merely

feelings, emotions—with

its instantaneous pleasure, indeed

so . . . exciting, in its space and place, but

Never

love . . . I remember

your tears what I thought

your pain—instead, just a

Game

and so, today the thoughts

of you are far and few . . . if ever

arising only as a—momentary

Memory

without any desire . . . shame

or blame for a feeling lost long

ago—to a love that never was, as

I

now enjoy the embracement

of a real love . . . that is warm, kind

friendly and a confidante—united in

Spirit

and soul . . . what a blessed grace is

true maturation—what exhilaration, what a

revelation . . . when one understands an empty

Heart

cannot be filled with materiality or physicality . . . and when

you believe in God's love so, too, will you receive and behold a

hallelujah—moment . . . with all its splendor and to Thee—I

Give

all the glory

say . . . thank You

for Your love and this love!

ALIKE

Oh, if

we only knew—every one

yes, you, me, them, they, he, she . . . etc., etc., etc.

are far more—alike than we realize . . . and that

Love is

the . . . primary element not only wanted but a . . . must in—order for

equality and equity to happen in its totality . . . so, the next time you focus

on another's differences with disrespect, distance, and demoralization try to

See self

and dare to explore beyond what you merely want to see or have others

see instead, check your shadow—yep, and you will undoubtedly . . . discover

an alikeness subsequently, growing taller, smarter, more compassionate,

knowledgeable, factual

And educated

regarding the truths . . . surrounding race relations, segregation, religion,

gender bias . . . discrimination with all its bigotries and hopefully, choose

to become a model: A legacy of a new . . . day simply called God—breathe

Knowledge power

and, thus, when we embrace, we acknowledge: When cut we all

eed, without water we all thirst, without food we will all be hungry, when

pain we all ache, when there is a storm we all seek shelter that is safe and

Welcoming as

is reflective of . . . His magnificent—gift of

parity, impartiality, neutrality, justice for all humanity and its overall

nvironment: Oh, the beauty of God's envisioned holy—likeness of us all!

SHADOWS

Black

white, green, blue, yellow, etc.

justice—sometimes truly, be blind to its

Human

race, face of enigma, symbolic of Judah

Joseph, Young, and Martin's Mountain—top

Foot

soldiers take up arms and they begin

yet, the enemy—disguised hard to sometimes detect and/or recognize

Who

thus, how to proceed, the battle has begun, the

blood . . . of a man, woman, child, or human race—who

sometimes only sees shadows of a crown . . . not a trace of

God

maybe our strategies are antique, weapons weak, or perhaps a

human race shall humble itself into victory when they not only

Know

His name, but . . . believe in Thy holy presence even

in battle, understanding . . . He is far more—powerful than any fight

Consequently

ictoriously, triumphantly, and gloriously when you let Him . . . in, follow

Iis—lead above all generals, not only shall you conquer the . . . battle, but

Win

ith—grace the ultimate . . . war in Thy holy name: If indeed we dare! What

immensity this blessing shall—be with shouts of Amen, Hallelujah, and

Praise

To

Thee...

MAGICAL

When

the heart—speaks

Listen

she is connecting to your

Gut

causing an entwinement—of

One's

soul and spirit—as if some

Supernatural

being is trying to get your—attention before you

Act

thus, heeding just might permit—space for . . . encouraging and

Allowing

a magical . . . spiritual—partnership of unity not just for the

Benefit

of self, but an—evolution . . . inspiring growth for all in its

Universe

what power, what beauty, what a revelation: What a holy—enchantment . .

OWN IT!

Normalizing

legitimizing, rationalizing, and looking

the other way of the deranged, bad . . . leadership and others who

follow just to get the little bones tossed to them selling . . . their

Souls

in exchange for and in support of . . . evil

inciting . . . violence and the like, some say this

is an absolute constitutional—crisis ruminating and

Radicalizing

surely, real souls . . . understand there is no getting

the genie—back in the bottle, instead to heal and move

forward . . . our leaders must not only have education, but a

Philosophy

personifying charismatics with a spirit of unification, objectivity

nd the ability to not only own—it but, do the . . . work to ensure that any

d all who engage in bad, destructive behaviors will be held . . . accountable

I

stand in

support . . . now

what about—you?

AFTERWORD

Well, this book . . . like all

of my books is compiled of poems that I have

written over several decades. One difference about this book

is that I had already . . . prepared it for copyright and print

when life . . . happened!

Yes, curve balls, thunderstorms, blizzards, hurricanes, heat

waves and the like! Oh, but . . . it is okay: You see, in spite of our time

on the clock, watch, radio, TV, cell phone, etc., the true . . . essence of

life—happens on God's . . . time!

And so, the birth of this book—breathes

life—today as is His . . . will and it feels good! What a

blessing. What else could it be when the Ultimate—Divine of

all time says . . . now!

So, with much—gratitude, I heard,

listened, and received this poetry . . . in motion

and—**SPIRITUAL WHISPERS** . . . was born!

"Always a Poet"

Bestselling Author

Dr. Jayé Wood

ACKNOWLEDGMENTS

Thank you: Sweet Jesus, My God and Lord—

that I Am . . . and because of You, I continue to be!

Hallelujah! Hallelujah! Hallelujah!

Thank you: Doris J. Cammack-Spencer—

for writing the foreword to this book. Your kindness and support shall endlessly fill my heart with . . . **gratitude** and **love!**

Thank you: Parish—

for your initial efforts to assist me with images. Then suddenly, I was without an image person. I was not sure in the essence of time . . . how I could get someone to step in quickly to complete the process. So, I prayed and simply gave it to God! Then low and behold, He sent me not one but two image persons: Bryanna (Lady B.) and Stan (The Man). For the **commitment** and **compassion** you both demonstrated, I not only **thank you,** but shall **treasure** your **kindness** and **support eternally!**

Thank you: Matthew—

for assisting me with the picture collage . . . I am forever **grateful!**

Thank you: Sir Duncan—

(my baby boy . . . my black lab)

Each day, regardless of the challenges that either of us have to endure, your love, compassion, and kindness never . . . waiver! Yes, with each awakening, I not only **thank God** for another day, but for you and the joy you continually bring to my life . . . every day! Whether together as I write, talking to others, riding in the car, strolling about your favorite pet store, walking (our daily morning two miles), or approaching construction workers, geek squad workers, mail or food deliverers, and neighbors, etc.—some just enjoying the newness of the day, some chatting with each other, some working in their yards, some leaving for work, and others having their morning walk, run, etc. Nevertheless, regardless of what they are doing, they often stop to take the . . . time to exchange good morning greetings with us and some even give you a warm pat or hug as—I wish them mutual greetings.

Then there are the various parked cars with children awaiting the school buses while waving and at least one or two getting out of the . . . car to pat and hug you while the other children gather nearby, standing in anticipation of the arrival of the school buses. Some giggle, laugh, and shout . . . with even a few jumping up and down saying, "It's Sir Duncan. Good morning, Sir Duncan," as I simultaneously wish them all a safe and wonderful day! Concurrently, the adults chime in, likewise, greeting us with mutual wishes! Yep, you always bring a smile, a laugh, and some joyfulness to others during these very challenging times!
What a **blessing** . . . indeed, **you—are!**

Thank you: Readers—

for taking this poetic journey. You are the best and I am—**grateful!**

HERE'S WHAT FOLKS ARE SAYING...

What a **blessed** opportunity to listen to Dr. Jayé's very **strong, confident**, and AMAZING poetic voice that **exudes** God's love throughout her book *SPIRITUAL WHISPERS*! How BEAUTIFUL! We **love** her! POWERFUL, INVIGORATING, and ENLIGHTENING were the words as she read through each poem. Dr. Jayé's poetic literacy when she speaks, without pushing or forcing, invites us all to experience this walk of faith, trust, and hope while sharing of her life's knowledge in such a **unique, profound**, and **masterful** poetic manner. Subsequently, one is able to quickly experience God's presence through her! I know we did! So deep are Dr. Jayé's poetic words with such **simplicity** that allows all to participate, **evolve**, and be **inspired** to **rise** above the rubble as she so **eloquently** speaks throughout her poetry.

Dr. Jayé, you are a **right on time poetic blessing** delivering a message of **kindness, caring, compassion, respect**, and **unity** with **equality** for all God's beings. We are still shouting, "**Hallelujah, amen**, and to **God** be the **glory**" for you! May God continue to guide and **bless** you to stay on this much-needed journey of HOPEFULNESS, teaching us that whether or not we are in the valley or a mountain, there must be an appreciation for them both in order that we might grow with appreciation to thy mighty God for each moment of each day, regardless of any challenges we may encounter. As Dr. Jayé makes clear throughout her poetry, God's light is always present. Just Let Him! Dr. Jayé, **thank you** for sharing your **Godly poetic gift!**

—Overseer/Pastor Javonn Bright, Co-Pastor Bryana Bright, Greater Gilgal Revival Center; Marietta, Georgia

Dr. Jayé Wood's book, *Spiritual Whispers*, touches on the most fundamental aspects of us as human beings—who are we, what is our purpose on this earth, and should we attain our goals at any cost to our fellow man or woman? As Dr. Jayé so POWERFULLY and **articulately** read the poems in this book, each poem **spoke to my heart** and emphasized what it means to be a good citizen in this world that is awash in chaos and controversy. As a person who travels and has family in other parts of the world, I thought *Spiritual Whispers* was speaking to Kenyans, where I originally come from, or Mexicans, where I have had the privilege of traveling. And surely it speaks to Americans and the overall world. Yes, Dr. Jayé is talking to all of us human beings as her **MIGHTY** poetic voice echoes: We are all the same irrespective of nationality, income level, race, or other factors. Life has its ups and downs, but we must be guided by compassion, family, fellowship, humility, and forgiveness. We are all one, and we should respect our fellow human beings irrespective of race or nationality.

Dr. Jayé has always **inspired** me and so many others through her writings, spoken words, integrity, and selflessness. My life is more prosperous by having known her, and *Spiritual Whispers* sums up who she is—**a poet of ministry**!

—Maina Muturi, Retired Economics Professor, Strayer University; Herndon, Virginia

I had the opportunity to attend a Zoom book reading of Dr. Jayé Wood's book, *Spiritual Whispers*. **WOW!** At the sound of Dr. Jayé's **POWERFUL, poetic voice**, I was immediately **mesmerized** and **lifted spiritually**! I believe that God created everyone as a **unique gift** as is obvious in the poetic words of Dr. Jayé as she **shares, encourages, motivates,** and **inspires** all of humanity to be kind and respectful of each other regardless of our differences!

In my experience, literature is often about the physical world; only a few people write about spiritual or metaphysical subjects. I **greatly appreciate and applaud** Dr. Jayé for taking the challenge to write about this abstract subject; thus, writing a **GREAT poetry** book for the **elevation** of people everywhere. This book is so needed during these challenging and chaotic times! Yes, I **greatly enjoyed** the book reading session and received something **positive** from all of the poems. Some of my favorite's that caused me to have an immediate **revelation** were:

"DIVINE WILL," "RIGHT," "ONLY YOU," "PLAY ON," "TRASH," "DADDY," and "DEHYDRATED," Dr. Jayé's poetry is so **unique** and

straightforward that if an individual just took a moment or so, even if in their leisure time, that person will find themselves a refined personality. The poetic views of Dr. Jayé are so **inspiring** that one feels **uplifted** listening to the **radiance** and **richness** of her voice as she reads these poems.

Dr. Jayé, **thank you** and may **God bless** your health with a prosperous future so that your writings continue to show a **right path** to us all, including the young generations.

—Amrik Singh Nagi; Accokeek, Maryland (born in Punjab, India)

Spiritual Whispers is a complication of poems **meticulously** created from the inner depths and soul of its author, Dr. Jayé Wood. Her poems touch people from all walks of life without any restrictions on age. Each chapter is full of **INSIGHTFUL** and **thought-provoking** poems that are guaranteed to strike up **stimulating** conversations relating to what we simply call life. The three parts of this book are building blocks that give one a taste and prepare us for a smorgasbord of **literary fulfillment**.

For example, in part one, the author's **ELOQUENT** and **STRONG** poetic voice quickly draws you in with an immediate **connection** and **revelation** of one's own life experiences in "BUTTERFLY TIME." "SIGNATURE" speaks to how God places a stamp on our lives from the very beginning to let us know we belong to Him and are covered in His protective care. "TRASH" speaks on the negativity we allow to infiltrate our lives, leaving a path of emotional and spiritual destruction. Then, Dr. Jayé effortlessly and with much **poetic grace** moves into part two which is comprised of **encouragement** to move past the hurt, overcome the enemy within, and let go of all your issues. Primarily, without pushing or demanding, Dr. Jayé is sharing and teaching how to overcome, stand strong, and let God do what He does best. Dr. Jayé finishes with part three, the finality of this **FASCINATING** trilogy, which focuses on inner strength, faith, and being a child of God. As her **lovely** poetic voice continued with **ease** and **confidence**, I was once again touched by all the poems like "DADDY," which is a favorite of mine. "I BELIEVE" and "ALIKE" caused a spiritual whisper to speak directly to me!

Dr. Jayé has done an **EXTRAORDINARY** job of **CAPTIVATING** her readers and challenging them without pushing anyone who may need to sometimes stop, pause, and maybe even ponder how they are living their life and if indeed it is consistent with their faith and belief in God! What a holy revelation this poetic reading has been for me! Dr. Jayé's poetry fills you but keeps you wanting **more! THANK YOU!**

—Anita M. Riley, Venue Manager, The American Legion Towson University Post #22; Baltimore, Maryland

It was a **pleasure** hearing Dr. Jayé read from her book, *Spiritual Whispers*. The **POWER** of her **poetic voice** grabs at your heart strings and **speaks to your spirit** saying the words that you need to hear. "Hope starts with you . . . and is contagious," "Witness the beauty of another's glow," and "Life is who you are" are just a few of the passages that **resonated** with me. It's a **very good** read and is ideal for anyone! Yes, the **universality** of Dr. Jayé's poetry is **AMAZING!**

—Yvette Mulkey, Communications Representative, Camp Springs, Maryland

Dr. Jayé Wood's book, *Spiritual Whispers*, is a **REMARKABLE** collection of poems with a string of **POWERFUL** messages of **HOPE** and humanity! As she read through the poems, her poetic voice was **STRONG** yet echoed **compassion**, **experience**, and **knowledge** with much **wisdom** which captured my immediate attention and caused me to reflect on my own life, to include the diversity of people that I see every day and how my staff and I could service them even better!

Thus, all of her poems caused me to have immediate **revelations**, reminding me that we are truly one! When she read "BUTTERFLY TIME," it spoke directly to me as it recapped how fleeting time is, how precious me could be, and how we take time for granted and waste it! Dr. Jayé, you are indeed an unexpected **poetic blessing** who is much-needed today!

—Dr. Ijeepomu Nwuju, Foot Specialist; Washington, D.C.

As a young woman in my 20s, Dr. Jayé Wood's poetry has **aspired** and **motivated** me to be a better person as it relates to always showing respect and being kind to others, which includes family, regardless of difference. I am blessed to have met Dr. Jayé, who has a very **UPLIFTING** soul, and I take pride in being chosen to share my thoughts about this **AMAZING** poet. When in doubt, Dr. Jayé's words remind me to keep going no matter what obstacle comes across my path.

Dr. Jayé, what a **blessing** you are to all humanity!

—Christina Calica, Veterinarian Assistant; Waldorf, Maryland

What a book of **INSPIRATION!** The soft yet powerful words of **love, kindness, resilience, perseverance, hope, belief,** and **faith** that echoed throughout Dr. Jayé's **POWERFUL** poetic voice as she read her poems, such as "LIFE" and "I BELIEVE" have allowed me the gratification of remembering who I am in this lifetime. *Spiritual Whispers* is something **new** and **refreshing** for both the **young** and **seasoned.**

Dr. Jayé, **thank you!** We are all **blessed** by your **gift** of **poetry** in **reality.** Dr. Jayé, you are **JUST WONDERFUL!**

—DvaStyl; Hollywood, Maryland

I had the **pleasure** and was likewise **HONORED** to participate in a reading of Dr. Jayé Wood's book, *Spiritual Whispers.* It was just REMARKABLE! I took a slice from each poem to make my own personal pie. In other words, each of the poems spiritually whispered to my spirit to strive to be the most spiritual and kind person I can be regardless of what I go through. I am glad to have had the opportunity to share this **lovely poetic gift** as Dr. Jayé so **eloquently** read each poem.

Thank you, Dr. Jayé for your *Spiritual Whispers.* **Amen!**

—C. M. Smith, Retired, Virginia Import Ltd; Springfield, Virginia

MORE PRAISE FOR THE AUTHOR

Dr. Jayé, your book, *Spiritual Whispers*, touches the soul and gives one a **POSITIVE** sense of what we can hear and receive when we take the time to listen to God's whispers. Your poems are extremely **MOTIVATIONAL** and **INSPIRATIONAL!** As I read your heartfelt poems, I found myself in a warm, serene place while at the same time realizing that many of these poems related to the whispering of my spirit. They opened a contact to the realm of my soul and **elevated** me to a higher place of **strength** causing me to reflect on a time when several of my family members were transiting from this life to the next. Also, the threads of your poetry so **eloquently** speak to enjoying and appreciating not only each day, but every minute. Likewise, providing **hope** and **encouragement** for all people regardless of their differences (including religions, opinions, etc.,) which is greatly needed during these very challenging times. You are truly a **gift**. Whether one has ever read poetry or not, there is something in this book for everyone—young and older. Your poetry is easy to read and beautifully laid out. Thus, upon opening the book, one immediately feels the **spirituality** of your poetry.

Dr. Jayé you are a **treasure, teacher,** and **preacher of poetic ministry!** Praise God, for you are **a blessing!**

—Founder Rev. Betty L. Steal, Love Fellowship Christian Ministries; Clinton, Maryland

Dr. Jayé Wood immediately captured my attention with her strong yet **GRACEFUL poetic voice** as she read from her book, *Spiritual Whispers*. While I enjoyed all the poems, some such as "DEAR GOD," "SAY WHAT," "JUDGEMENTALITY," and "THE STORM" are very relatable, particularly to my own life. An **INSPIRING** message of **authenticity** pervades throughout her poetry! It is as if Dr. Jayé is providing a form of **spiritual direction** for all humanity during these sometimes catastrophic times. Ultimately, as she read her poetry, the words seemed to say, "Trust in God and things will always work out!"

Dr. Jayé is without a doubt a **motivator, master educator**, and surely a **poetic minister!** Yes, Dr. Jayé, you are a **GIFT** of a **BLESSING** to many, which includes me, and I **thank you!**

—D. Novel, Transdermal Operator; Brooklyn, New York

I had the **HONOR** of participating in a reading of Dr. Jayé Wood's book, *Spiritual Whispers*, and her ability to **INSPIRE** others, both young and old, through her poetry is an **AMAZING GRACE!** Her poetic voice has a **calmness** and **simplicity**; thus, one has no hesitation when trying to figure out the author's meanings. Instead, her words are very clear and easy to comprehend! It was a **talent** that I have never experienced before from any poetic reading, and it allowed myself and others to not only stay focused on Dr. Jayé's poetic message but quickly grasp and revisit our own life experiences of highs and lows. For example, poems like "SHADOWBOXING" spoke to me directly and reminded me of my younger self—relentless, clueless, and fearless. "TRASH" encourages one to rise above the toxicity of haters, naysayers, jealousy, and envy and teaches acceptance of diversities by encouraging equality and equity for all God's people!

I truly **enjoyed** Dr. Jayé's poetic reading and was in **awe** at how these poems really hit home for me. Overall, these poems **motivate** one to do better while instantaneously **uplifting** their self-esteem. Likewise, permeated throughout Dr. Jayé's **POWERFUL POETRY** is her **warm** and **engaging** poetic voice which **encourages** finding acceptance in self, smiling through the pain, and **aspiring** an **elevation** of self while simultaneously **lifting** others and always letting God in.

Dr. Jayé, may you continue this **holy** journey with **peace, love,** and **blessings always! Thank you** and much **praise!**

—Mak Massillon, Vice-President and Financial Advisor, Truist Investment Services; Silver Spring, Maryland

I am truly **HONORED** that Dr. Jayé Wood allowed me to participate in her book reading of *Spiritual Whispers*. Unequivocally, it was a **MASTERCLASS!** In other words, during Dr. Jayé's poetic reading, her ability to capture everyone's attention as she expertly taught through her **poetic penning** with such skillfulness as she reads each poem was **masterful!** This coupled with the etchings of her **graceful** yet very **POWERFUL poetic** voice was **ASTONISHING!** It left an imprint on my mind that still resonates **profoundly** long after the reading! I truly enjoyed all the poems which **personified** a common thread to society and all its challenges today with advice, suggestions, and directions for improving one's life. Just to name a few of the **BRILLIANT** poems read by Dr. Jayé, "JOY" spoke directly to me as it relates to hearing and listening to the spiritual whispers and living your dreams. "SHADOWBOXING" spoke of not just looking at the shadow in the mirror but having the courage to look beyond it, and "FALSE FACE" addressed judging others while faking a good life!

Dr. Jayé, **THANK YOU** for imparting some of your wisdom to hopefully inspire and motivate others to grow beyond their status quo and become the unique gift God created them to be! What an **AMAZING POETIC GIFT** God has given you! I cannot wait to see where the next chapter in your life takes you! Wishing you much future **success** in all you do with **God's vision** of the **gift He** has bestowed upon you!

—James E. Smith, ABC News Engineer; Washington, D.C.

Spiritual Whispers reads like a personal narrative. It's as if Dr. Jayé Wood's soul flows through the pages of this book so I could fully understand and appreciate all the complexities of life. From putting on a "FALSE FACE" in one poem to learning about "JOY" in another to simply defining what it means to be "FOOT SOLDIERS," Dr. Jayé's poems are **AUTHENTIC, AMAZING,** and **BEAUTIFUL**. They will surely aid those needing to know what it means to find a spiritual and mental sense of self, particularly during today's intricate times, and hopefully encourage us all to stay on the "right path" as Dr. Jayé so **eloquently** and poetically puts it!

Thank you, Dr. Jayé, for sharing this lovely **SPIRITUAL GIFT** of **INSPIRATION** for all humanity!

—Anita Stewart-Hammerer M.S., Commander, The American Legion Towson University Post #22; Baltimore, Maryland

Dr. Jayé Wood writes poetry for everyone! She embraces and encourages equity and equality for all people, regardless of differences, throughout her poetry. Such a **UNIQUE POETIC VOICE!** The simplicity yet **profoundness** of Dr. Jaye's poetry allows all to engage, enjoy, grow, and **inspire** others to do the same! I truly enjoyed all of the poems! "LOOKIN GOOD" highlighted that when one feels good on the inside, they not only look good, but they can bring a needed smile to another. "TRASH" spoke to moving above the debris in order to birth our dreams. "FLIP" talked about flipping the script in one's own life, much like a light switch. Then, "PLAY ON," **wow!** I can still hear the **strength** and **wisdom** of Dr. Jaye's **POWERFUL** poetic voice saying, ". . . this play is—yours…" Simply **MESMERIZING!**

Dr. Jayé, may God allow you to continue this journey of sharing realistic poetry to **motivate** and **lift** others not only to **rise** above today's rubble an injustices, but to appreciate **His light** which surely **shines** through you. **CONGRATULATIONS** and **well done! Thank you!**

—Al Bratton, Tax & Business Strategies, PC Attorney/CPA; Largo, Maryland

Dr. Jaye's Brother Douglas

Dr. Jaye' with Brother Joseph

Dr. Jaye' with Sister Rosenarie

Dr. Jaye's Niece Patrice

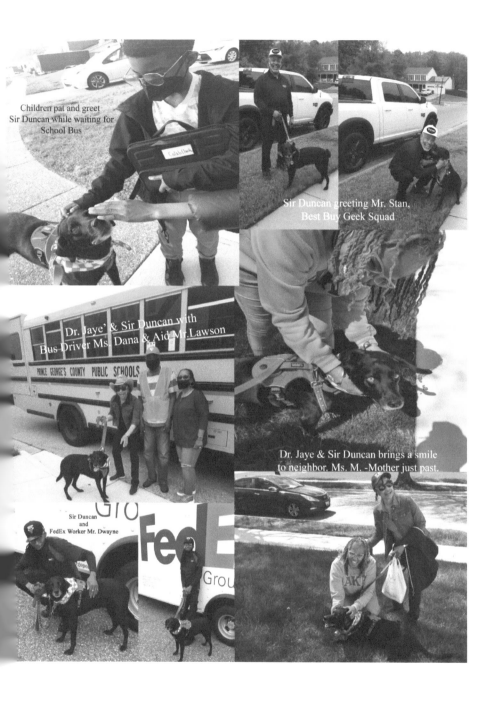

Children pat and greet Sir Duncan while waiting for School Bus

Sir Duncan greeting Mr. Stan, Best Buy Geek Squad

Dr. Jaye' & Sir Duncan with Bus Driver Ms. Dana & Aid Mr. Lawson

PRINCE GEORGE'S COUNTY PUBLIC SCHOOLS

Dr. Jaye & Sir Duncan brings a smile to neighbor, Ms. M. -Mother just past.

Sir Duncan and FedEx Worker Mr. Dwayne

I LOVE HEARING FROM YOU!

Over the years, I have received many positive responses to my poetry from readers. I am always pleased that my poetry continues to serve as inspiration, healing, affirmation, and relaxation for so many. I welcome your positive comments. They might be used for publication; therefore, please indicate at the end of your comment, "You may use for publication."

Please send comments to:

Dr. Jayé Wood, Always a Poet,

9134 Piscataway Road

P.O. Box 2069

Clinton, Maryland, 20735

Email: alwaysapoet0920@gmail.com

Website: alwaysapoet.com

ABOUT THE AUTHOR

Dr. Jayé Wood is the founder and CEO of JAYE' ASSOCIATES, a motivational speaker, and a presenter. Referred to by many as a poetic minister and minister of kindness, Dr. Jayé is a beacon of hope and inspiration.

Dr. Jayé has worked in higher education as a dean and professor in organizational leadership, psychology, and criminal justice. She previously served as an executive assistant to the director of community correctional services at the DC Department of Corrections and a liaison for the corporation counsel, superior court, and federal bureau of prisons. During this time, she coordinated the city's halfway houses and developed and implemented the first electronic monitoring program for ex-offenders and served as a supervisor for the Special Temporary Employment Program for Ex-Offenders (STEP) in Washington, DC.

Learn more at alwaysapoet.com.

CREATING DISTINCTIVE BOOKS
WITH INTENTIONAL RESULTS

We're a collaborative group of creative masterminds
with a mission to produce high-quality books to position
you for monumental success in the marketplace.

Our professional team of writers, editors, designers,
and marketing strategists work closely together to ensure
that every detail of your book is a clear representation
of the message in your writing.

Want to know more?
Write to us at info@publishyourgift.com
or call (888) 949-6228

Discover great books, exclusive offers, and more at
www.PublishYourGift.com

Connect with us on social media

@publishyourgift

Lightning Source UK Ltd.
Milton Keynes UK
UKHW052027030123
414791UK00001B/2